T0407095

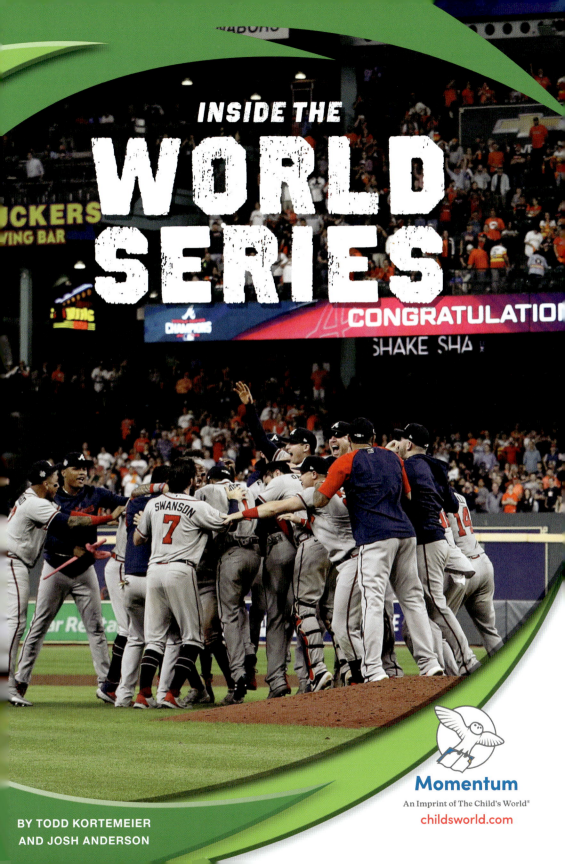

INSIDE THE
WORLD SERIES

Momentum

An Imprint of The Child's World®

childsworld.com

BY TODD KORTEMEIER
AND JOSH ANDERSON

ABOUT THE AUTHORS

Josh Anderson lives in the Los Angeles area with his two sons and a giant dog. He's been to tons of sporting events, but his favorite was seeing sumo wrestling in Tokyo, Japan.

Todd Kortemeier is a writer and journalist from Minneapolis. He is a graduate of the University of Minnesota's School of Journalism & Mass Communication.

Published by The Child's World®
800-599-READ • www.childsworld.com

Photography Credits
Cover: ©Carmen Mandato / Staff / Getty Images; page 1: ©Carmen Mandato / Staff / Getty Images; page 5: ©Elsa / Staff / Getty Images; page 6: ©Jennifer Stewart / Stringer / Getty Images; page 9: ©Alex Trautwig / Stringer / Getty Images; page 10: ©Julie Denesha / Stringer / Getty Images; page 13: ©Elsa / Staff / Getty Images; page 14: ©Bob Levey / Stringer / Getty Images; page 16: ©Patrick McDermott / Stringer / Getty Images; page 19: ©Rich Pilling / Stringer / Getty Images; page 21: ©Bettmann / Contributor / Getty Images; page 22: ©Rich Pilling / Contributor / Getty Images; page 24: ©Carmen Mandato / Staff / Getty Images; page 26: ©Carmen Mandato / Staff / Getty Images; page 27: ©Carmen Mandato / Staff / Getty Images; page 28: ©Tom Pennington / Staff / Getty Images

ISBN Information
9781503865204 (Reinforced Library Binding)
9781503866201 (Portable Document Format)
9781503867048 (Online Multi-user eBook)
9781503867888 (Electronic Publication)

LCCN 2022940585

Printed in the United States of America

CONTENTS

FAST FACTS

▶ The World Series is the championship of Major League Baseball (MLB). The winners of the National League (NL) and American League (AL) play each other. The series is best-of-seven games. The first team to win four games is the winner.

▶ The winning team has received the **Commissioner's** Trophy since 1967. The trophy is made of silver and gold. It is around 30 inches (76 cm) high. There are 30 flags attached to its base. Each flag has the name of an MLB team.

▶ The World Series begins in late October. It is also known as the Fall Classic. Sometimes it stretches into November.

▶ The World Series is played at the home ballparks of both teams playing for the championship.

▶ The first World Series was played in 1903. It started as a best-of-nine series. The Boston Americans beat the Pittsburgh Pirates, winning five games to three.

▶ World Series games draw big crowds. Through 2021, the World Series game with the highest attendance was a 1959 battle between the Los Angeles Dodgers and the Chicago White Sox. Almost 93,000 people attended Game 5 at Los Angeles Memorial Coliseum.

CHAPTER ONE

A MANAGER'S PERSPECTIVE: DAVE ROBERTS

As a player, Dave Roberts played a big role on the 2004 Boston Red Sox. That team won its first World Series in 86 years.

The Los Angeles Dodgers hired Roberts as their manager before the 2016 season. Fans in LA were hungry for success. They hoped he could lead their team to its first World Series victory since 1988. Roberts wanted to win as a manager, just like he had as a player.

"To be able to wear the Dodgers uniform and represent this world-class organization on and off the field, is truly an honor," Roberts said. [1]

◀ **Dave Roberts played Major League Baseball for 10 years before becoming a manager.**

The team finished first in the National League West division after each of Roberts' first four seasons in charge. He even led the team to the World Series in 2017 and 2018. But the Dodgers lost both times.

The World Series loss in 2018 was to Roberts' former team, the Red Sox. Afterward, Roberts tried to keep his players and fans focused on all they had achieved. "To say we didn't win a championship, and to say it was an unsuccessful season, I think that's doing a disservice to everyone in that clubhouse," he said.[2]

The Dodgers made it to the World Series again in 2020. Their opponent was the Tampa Bay Rays. The Dodgers and Rays had both finished the regular season with the most wins in their league.

Dodgers ace pitcher Clayton Kershaw led his team to victory in Game 1. Then, the teams traded wins over the next four games. The Dodgers led three games to two. A win in Game 6 meant they'd be champions.

The Rays scored right away and took a 1–0 lead after the first inning. But that was the only run Tampa Bay would score for the night. The Dodgers scored three runs later in the game. They won 3–1. Roberts had finally brought a World Series victory to Los Angeles.

▲ **The Dodgers have finished first in the National League West for five seasons under Dave Roberts.**

With the victory, Roberts became the first manager of Asian heritage to win the World Series. His mother is Japanese American.

"To know that we brought a championship back to Los Angeles and no one can ever take it away, I'm just so proud of our guys," Roberts said.[3]

CHAPTER TWO

A FAN'S PERSPECTIVE: ROYALS FANS

The fan's sign read, "This is really happening!"

The sign spoke for thousands of Kansas City Royals fans. Thousands were watching Game 4 of the 2014 American League Championship Series (ALCS) at Kauffman Stadium, the team's home park. Thousands more were glued to their TVs at home. Others were at a big party in downtown Kansas City. When Royals third baseman Mike Moustakas threw to first base for the final out, all the fans felt it. It was something they had not felt since 1985. Broadcaster Denny Matthews said it all.

"Kansas City, you've got a World Series."[4]

The Royals had swept the Baltimore Orioles to become AL champions. For some fans, it had been a lifetime of waiting. Phillip Zeeck was two when the Royals won it all in 1985.

◄ **Royals fans came out in full force for their team's magical run to the 2014 World Series.**

The team had not been back to the World Series since. Zeeck did not expect the Royals to make it back. He also did not think he would be there when they did.

The years of waiting were worth it. Walking into Kauffman Stadium, Zeeck had never seen it so full and energetic.

"They could lose tomorrow night, and then win the next dozen World Series, and it still wouldn't feel as good as this moment," Zeeck said.[5]

Milton Johnson was 12 in 1985. In 2014, he had a 12-year-old son of his own. They attended the World Series with Milton's father, Milton Sr. Three generations of Johnson men experienced their first Fall Classic game together.

Royals fans everywhere were excited. But fan SungWoo Lee probably traveled the farthest to support the team.

Lee was from South Korea. He became hooked after seeing a Royals highlight on TV. He was amazed by Kauffman Stadium. The Royals had had just one winning season since he had started watching as a middle-school student in the 1990s. But Lee stuck with them. He attended his first Royals game in August 2014. When the Royals made the World Series, Lee had to be there.

The first time he visited, the Royals swept the San Francisco Giants in the regular season. The two teams met again in the 2014 World Series. Lee was confident history would repeat itself. But the Royals lost 7–1 in Game 1. Lee still believed.

▲ Superfan SungWoo Lee made the trip from South Korea to Kansas City to watch his beloved Royals in the World Series.

"The Royals made a great comeback victory in the **Wild Card** Game, from 7–3, and won that game," he said. "So I still believe we can make it. I believe the Royals will win the World Series."[6]

But belief was not enough. The Royals lost in seven games. The fans were disappointed. But they were still proud. After the last out in Game 7, as the Giants celebrated on the infield of Kauffman Stadium, a cheer rose from the crowd.

"Thank you, Royals," the fans chanted.[7]

CHAPTER THREE

THE GM'S PERSPECTIVE: MIKE RIZZO

Mike Rizzo grew up around the game of baseball. The sport was almost like a "family business." His father and grandfather were both scouts. Baseball scouts travel around trying to find talented players for their teams. Rizzo became a scout as well. Then, he played and coached baseball.

Rizzo became Washington's general manager (GM) in 2009. The Nationals hadn't finished with a winning record in five seasons. They had also never won a World Series. Rizzo tried to bring a new outlook with him to the job.

A baseball team's manager makes decisions on the field each day. The GM's responsibility is to sign players and make trades. A GM's goal is to give the manager the best team possible each season. Rizzo believed in making sure his good players were also good people.

◄ **Mike Rizzo places the Commissioner's Trophy in his windowsill of his Washington, DC, home to celebrate baseball's Opening Day each spring.**

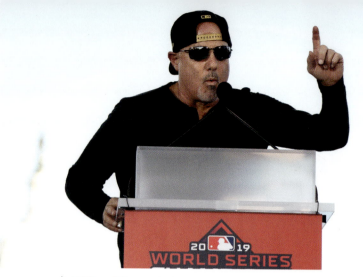

▲ **Mike Rizzo joined the Nationals in 2007, two years after the team moved from Montreal, Canada, to Washington, DC.**

"He's huge on **chemistry** and clubhouse stuff, not bringing in bad teammates, not bringing in bad guys," said Ryan Zimmerman, a Nationals player.[8]

It took Rizzo a few seasons to turn the Nationals into a successful team. He built the team's **minor league** system by signing skilled young players who could help the Nationals one day. In 2012, Washington finished in first place and earned a trip to the playoffs. They reached the playoffs four more times from 2013 to 2018.

Almost all of the players on the 2019 Washington Nationals had been signed or **drafted** during Rizzo's time as the team's GM. That year, the Nationals earned a spot in the World Series. Rizzo watched players he'd drafted as teenagers, like Juan Soto, compete with the Houston Astros for a championship.

The team Rizzo built won the first two games of the 2019 World Series. But the Astros came back to win the next three. Houston was one win away from denying Washington a World Series victory. Then, the Nationals battled back and won the next two games. They were champions.

The winning pitcher in Game 7 was Patrick Corbin. Rizzo signed Corbin before the 2019 season. Stephen Strasburg was named the World Series' Most Valuable Player. Rizzo helped to draft Strasburg when he was the team's assistant GM.

Rizzo was given a great honor after the Nationals' World Series victory. He was named 2019's Major League Executive of the Year.

Even in such a big moment, he couldn't help but think once more about baseball as the family business. "Dad is the reason I'm here," he said. "He's forgotten more baseball than I know."[9]

DEADLINE FOR DEALS

Baseball's trade deadline usually falls around July 31. After the deadline, certain rules make it much harder for teams to make trades. In the weeks before the deadline, general managers are very busy. Their goal is to make their team better for the rest of the season and the playoffs. Teams that have hopes of winning the World Series often trade promising minor league players for talented major leaguers.

CHAPTER FOUR

AN UMPIRE'S PERSPECTIVE: DON DENKINGER

Don Denkinger never wanted to be an umpire. He played sports in high school and college in Iowa. But baseball was not his game. Denkinger had planned to go back to college after serving two years in the US Army. But a friend asked him to instead attend an umpire school.

"I couldn't even fathom what it was an umpire was supposed to do," Denkinger said.[10]

It turned out Denkinger had quite a knack for it. He was the best student at the school. He then became one of the top umpires in baseball. He umpired four World Series in his career.

Don Denkinger spent three ▶ decades as an MLB umpire.

But he is best remembered for a mistake. Denkinger was umpiring at first base during Game 6 of the 1985 World Series. The St. Louis Cardinals were up 3–2 in the series over the Kansas City Royals. It was the ninth inning. The Cardinals were up 1–0. They were three outs away from winning the World Series.

Royals pinch hitter Jorge Orta hit a soft groundball to first. Cardinals pitcher Todd Worrell covered the base. First baseman Jack Clark fielded the ball and threw to Worrell. The ball was high and a little behind Worrell, but the 6-foot-5-inch **reliever** caught it. Denkinger was behind the base in foul territory. He was looking right at the play.

Maybe it was the crowd noise. Or maybe Denkinger was too close and could not watch the ball and the base at the same time. Denkinger called Orta safe. But the ball had beaten Orta by half a step. The Cardinals bench erupted.

"We can't seem to draw a break," Cardinals manager Whitey Herzog yelled at Denkinger.[11]

Denkinger would not change his call. He did not find out he was wrong until after the game. That was when he asked Commissioner Peter Ueberroth if his call had been right.

"And he just shook his head no," Denkinger said. "That's when I knew that I missed it. I couldn't have felt more sick."[12]

Cardinals reliever Todd Worrell (38) ▶ argues with Denkinger in the ninth inning of Game 6 of the 1985 World Series.

▲ The Kansas City Royals celebrate their
first ever World Series title.

After Orta was called safe, the Cardinals fell apart. They made defensive mistakes and pitched poorly. The Royals won 2–1. Herzog was livid. He blamed Denkinger for the loss.

To make matters worse, Denkinger was going to be behind home plate for Game 7.

The Royals destroyed the Cardinals, who were perhaps still reeling from the blown call, 11–0 to win the series. St. Louis fans blamed Denkinger. They sent him hate mail and placed angry phone calls to his home. Denkinger felt terrible. But he knew the Cardinals' loss was not his fault.

"I love baseball and I'm not all that disillusioned by what's happened to me," he said later. "I'll continue to do what I've always done, which is to take every game very seriously and do my best."[13]

CHAPTER FIVE

A PLAYER'S PERSPECTIVE: MAX FRIED

Max Fried's greatest moment on a baseball field almost didn't happen.

The young left-hander had been lucky. He had pitched in the playoffs in three of his first five seasons. In 2021, Fried's Atlanta Braves won the National League Championship Series. That meant they were going to the World Series.

Fried was one of Atlanta's top pitchers in 2021. The Braves won Game 1 against the Houston Astros. Fried was chosen as the team's **starting pitcher** for Game 2.

He tried to have a positive attitude going into the game. "You have to really trust the work and the preparation that you've put up until this point," he said.[14]

◄ **Max Fried made his MLB debut in 2017 with the Atlanta Braves.**

▲ **Max Fried won the National League's Gold Glove Award for pitching in 2020 and 2021.**

Unfortunately, Fried's first World Series game didn't go as planned. He gave up six runs during his five innings. The Braves lost the game 7–2. The loss allowed the Astros to tie the series. Each team now had a win.

The Braves won two of the next three games. Fried's team was one win away from a championship. Then, Fried got another chance. He was picked as the starting pitcher in Game 6.

Fried warmed up with catcher Travis d'Arnaud before the game. D'Arnaud could tell that Fried's pitches looked better than they had before Game 2. "He was drilling every pitch," d'Arnaud said. "He had it."[15]

▲ **Max Fried throws five different kinds of pitches for the Braves, including a 94 MPH (151 KPH) fastball.**

GETTING A GRIP

Major leaguers throw many different kinds of pitches. A fastball looks very different to a hitter than a curveball. And a slider behaves differently than a knuckleball. How a pitcher positions his fingers on the ball greatly affects the way it moves when thrown. Even which part of the ball's seams the pitcher touches will change the way it moves toward the batter.

▲ The 2021 World Series win was the
fourth in Atlanta Braves history.

The second batter Fried faced in the game hit a soft ground ball to the Braves' first baseman. Fried ran over to cover first base. The Astros' runner accidentally stepped on his ankle. It looked like the pitcher was hurt. He walked back toward the pitcher's mound with a limp.

Braves' manager Brian Snitker and a trainer ran out to check on Fried. The pitcher told them he was fine to stay in the game.

"It didn't feel good," Fried said later. "But at that point—it's the World Series. You've just got to figure out how to get through."[16]

Fried did better than "get through" the rest of the game. He only gave up four hits in six innings. He didn't allow a single run. The Braves won the game 7–0. They were Major League Baseball's 2021 champions.

"To be able to get a little bit of a redo after Game 2, I just wanted to make the most of it," Fried said after the game. "I just wanted to leave everything out there."[17]

THINK ABOUT IT

► What can make a star athlete have a terrible game?
► Many fans are loyal to their team even in a losing season. What do you think keeps fans coming back year after year?
► Many great athletes become coaches or managers when they stop playing. How does playing a sport help someone become a great coach?

GLOSSARY

chemistry (KEM-ess-tree): To have chemistry on a team means that the players, coaches, and managers get along well with each other.

commissioner (kuh-MISH-uh-ner): The commissioner is the person in charge of Major League Baseball. The commissioner presents the winning team with the World Series trophy.

drafted (DRAFT-ed): Players are drafted when teams select them to join their organization.

minor league (MY-nur LEEG): The minor league is one level below Major League Baseball. The players are professionals associated with a major league team, but they are still considered in training and are preparing for major league play.

reliever (reh-LEEV-ur): A reliever is a pitcher who comes into a game after the starting pitcher.

starting pitcher (START-ing PICH-er): A starting pitcher plays from the beginning of the game. Max Fried is a great starting pitcher for the Braves.

Wild Card (WILD KARD): The two teams with the best records in their leagues that do not win their divisions make the playoffs as Wild Card teams. The 2014 Royals were a Wild Card team.

SOURCE NOTES

1. Dodger Blue, "2020 World Series: Dave Roberts explains mishandling of Pedro Baez in Dodgers' walk-off loss," YouTube Video, 6:16, October 24, 2020, https://www.youtube.com/watch?v=_6kmPghrbc0

2. Daniel Starkand. "Dave Roberts Expects Dodgers To Win 2019 World Series." Dodger Blue. Medium Large Sports Media. 31 Oct. 2018.

3. ESPN, "Dave Roberts calls Dodgers winning World Series 'surreal' | SportsCenter," YouTube Video, 4:48, October 27, 2020, https://www.youtube.com/watch?v=W-0bN66uO84

4. Andrew Lynch. "World Series-Bound Royals: Appreciating Fans, Family." Fox 4 KC. Tribune Broadcasting. 16 Oct. 2014. Web. 6 Apr. 2015.

5. Erin Faulk. "Long-Awaited World Series Run Brings Generations of Royals Fans Together." Sporting News. Sporting News Media. 29 Oct. 2014. Web. 6 Apr. 2015.

6. Ted Berg. "Royals' South Korean Superfan Sung Woo Lee Reflects on Incredible Year." USA Today. Gannett Company. 21 Oct. 2014. Web. 6 Apr. 2015.

7. Ricky Doyle. "Kansas City Fans Chant 'Thank You, Royals' After World Series Loss (Video)." NESN. New England Sports Network. 30 Oct. 2014. Web. 6 Apr. 2015.

8. Chelsea Janes. "Mike Rizzo built contending Nationals teams before, but 'personally, I needed to get here.'" The Washington Post. Nash Holdings. 31 Oct. 2019.

9. Lacy Lusk. "2019 MLB Executive Of The Year: Mike Rizzo." Baseball America. Baseball America Enterprises. 3 Dec. 2019.

10–11. Ron Fimrite. "In the Eye of the Storm." Sports Illustrated. Time Inc. 6 Jan. 1986. Web. 7 Apr. 2015.

12. Sean Gregory. "The Ump Who Blew the '85 World Series Wants a Rematch." Time. Time Inc. 14 Oct. 2014. Web. 7 Apr. 2015.

13. Ron Fimrite. 6 Jan. 1986.

14. Jesse Sanchez. "Fried's focus on control as Braves' G2 starter." MLB.com. MLB Advanced Media. 27 Oct. 2021.

15–16. Emma Baccellieri. "Max Fried Finds Another Level to Win One for the Braves and Starters Everywhere." SI.com. ABG-SI, LLC. 3 Nov. 2021.

17. Matt Snyder. "Max Fried dazzles with six shutout innings in World Series Game 6 as Braves take home first title since 1995." CBSSports.com. CBS Interactive.3 Nov. 2021.

TO LEARN MORE

BOOKS

Goodman, Michael E. *The Story of the Atlanta Braves.* Mankato, MN: Creative Education, 2021.

Herman, Gail. *What Is the World Series?* New York: Grosset & Dunlap, 2019.

Jacobs, Greg. *The Everything Kids' Baseball Book.* Avon, MA: Adams Media, 2020.

WEBSITES

Visit our website for links about baseball: **childsworld.com/links**

Note to Parents, Caregivers, Teachers, and Librarians: We routinely verify our web links to make sure they are safe and active sites. So encourage your readers to check them out!

INDEX